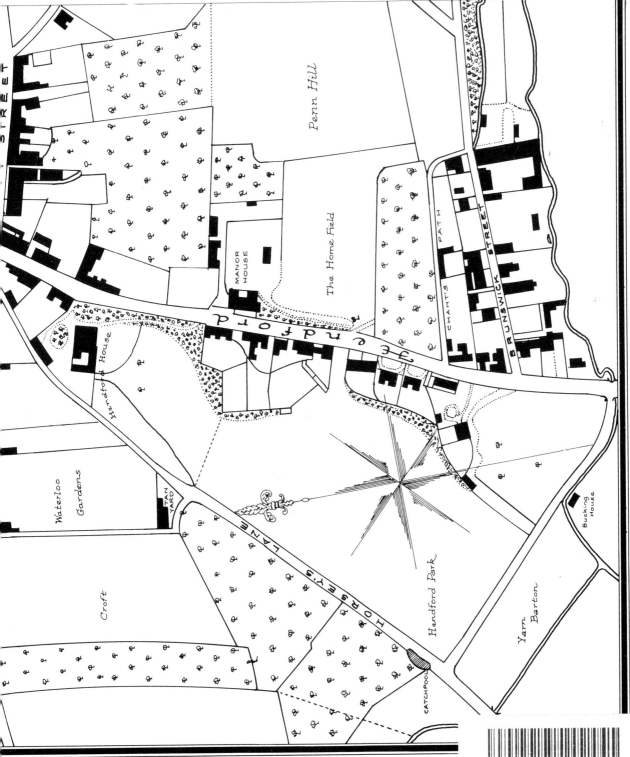

South-west section of Yeovil 1831, redrawn and adapted from a survey by E. Watts.

YESTERDAY'S YEOVIL

'NORTH' (KINGSTON) TURNPIKE GATE, c1875. From a photograph by T. Clarke, a Gloucester photographer.

THE GEORGE HOTEL, MIDDLE STREET.

YESTERDAY'S
YEOVIL

a sketchbook of places past

BY

LESLIE BROOKE

BARRACUDA BOOKS LIMITED
BUCKINGHAM, ENGLAND
MCMLXXXIX

PUBLISHED BY BARRACUDA BOOKS LIMITED
BUCKINGHAM, ENGLAND
AND PRINTED BY
H. E. BODDY & COMPANY LIMITED
BANBURY, ENGLAND

BOUND BY
CEDRIC CHIVERS LIMITED
BATH, ENGLAND

JACKET PRINTED BY
CHENEY & SONS LIMITED
BANBURY, OXON

LITHOGRAPHY BY
FORE COLOUR GRAPHICS LIMITED
HERTFORD, ENGLAND

DISPLAY SET IN BASKERVILLE
AND TEXT SET IN 10½/12pt BASKERVILLE BY
KEY COMPOSITION
NORTHAMPTON, ENGLAND

ISBN 0 86023 450 9

CONTENTS

PREFACE *by His Worship The Mayor of Yeovil, John Cruddas*

It is with pleasure, and a sense of *déjà vu*, that I write this introduction to Leslie Brooke's latest work on Yeovil, the many illustrations for which consist entirely of his own meticulously executed pen and ink drawings. I say *déjà vu*, since I was also Mayor when his highly successful *Book of Yeovil* was published in 1978, and for which I also contributed the preface.

Even during the comparatively short period which has elapsed between these two books, Yeovil has seen a great many changes, and it is surprising how quickly one forgets how certain locations appeared previously. Leslie has covered changes ranging over a period of some 200 years in a 'walk' through the town's streets, not only recalling what once the scene was like and adding an anecdote here and there, but also pointing out many features which still remain, while adding a few modern examples, not all of which, one must admit, can be said to exhibit the same pleasing appearance as some now disappeared.

In commending this book, may I modestly refer to the careful renovation of a building of character, included in this book, namely the Town House in Union Street, built by Town Commissioners in 1849, which fittingly has now become the home of Yeovil Town Council.

John Cruddas.

DEDICATION

For Marjorie, Peter and David.

FOREWORD *by David Young RIBA MSIA AIArb FRSA*

It was not so long ago that you could buy a proper pint of beer with real money — I mean shillings and pence; those were the days when steam trains ran in and out of Yeovil Town Station (now a car park) and Pen Mill Station (just still with us). When our real values were the Old Values; days of Grammar Schools and cash transactions, when sums were worked out on paper with an ink pen (not your ball-point of today) and not on calculators which leave many of us confused. I speak to my son of such days with fond affection and he laughs at me in much the same way as I laughed at my father when he reminisced of horses and carts, and shoes which were repaired again and again rather than being thrown away after just a few wearings.

It is of such days that Leslie Brooke writes and so beautifully illustrates with his wonderful pen and ink drawings. *Yesterday's Yeovil* is a veritable feast of nostalgia, covering some two hundred years of the Town's history and buildings.

I have been privileged to know Leslie Brooke as a neighbour, colleague and friend for half a century and throughout that time he has been recording Yeovil's fascinating history for future generations. They, no doubt, will be asking the question, not so much what were shillings and pence, but what was a pint of beer?!

We in Yeovil are lucky to have a man of his multiple talents among us. Leslie, we thank you and are very grateful.

David Young

FORMER COTTAGES, PRESTON PLUCKNETT

'ABBEY FARM' AND BARN, PRESTON PLUCKNE

YESTERDAY'S YEOVIL

And shall this venerated pile
  For ever pass away
And no regret, nor sigh be raised,
  Not e'en this simple lay?

May something noble take its place
  To grace the cherish'd spot,
But no mean, worthless structure raise
  To form a lasting blot.

These, the final two of eight verses written on the demolition in 1850 of Yeovil's Market House, which had occupied a site in the centre of 'The Borough', may serve as the *raison d'être* for this volume. In these pages will be found many once-familiar scenes, a few of which remain more or less intact, though sadly others have been mutilated, yet more have only bits and pieces surviving, and the majority have gone for ever. A few modern examples are included, in order that the reader can assess whether the sentiments expressed in the last verse have been realised.

Until 1808, regular perambulations of parish boundaries took place in order to impress them on the minds of those taking part, particularly the younger generation. Changes in landmarks would then be noted, and in some respects the drawings and text which follow, will attempt to serve a similar purpose. Scenes of yesterday will be recalled, following a somewhat tortuous route, starting on the outskirts on one side of the town, then journeying through the centre to finish on the opposite side.

Starting at Preston, the drawing of thatched cottages not so long ago standing close to the church of St James, is just one example of how much its one-time rural appearance has been transformed since 1928 boundary extensions incorporated the village into the borough. On the other hand, just a matter of yards — one ought to say metres now, I suppose — down the road, the Abbey Farm retains much of the character shown in the drawing, before it became the headquarters of the firm of building contractors and developers. Really 'Preston Great Farm', it was renamed by Lady Georgiana Fane, who inherited the estate in 1841, in the mistaken belief that it had been the property of the Priory of Bermondsey.

11

YEOVIL UNION PUBLIC ASSISTANCE INSTITUTION, PRESTON ROAD, BUILT 1837.

Moving on towards the town, Summerlands Hospital administration block, facing the road, was part of Yeovil Workhouse, or the Union Public Assistance Institution, to give its more impressive official designation. Built in 1837, with room for 300 paupers, accommodation was later provided for sixty sick patients. The inmates wore fustian jackets, waistcoats, and trousers, with ribbed worsted stockings, and were also given neckerchiefs. Converted into a hospital, it was opened by Sir John English in 1973.

Crossing Westfield Road (here was once a brickyard), Grovecote now stands flanked by more modern dwellings, but it was built in 1830 as a manse for the Unitarian minister of that time. Legion Road is built over part of the grounds of Grove House, former headquarters of the local branch of the British Legion, but only a pillar of its entrance gates now remains.

Just past the cemetery gates is the Quaker burial ground of 1694, at that time well outside the town's limits. The construction of the Fiveways roundabout necessitated the cutting back of a considerable amount of ground at the bottom of Ilchester Road. On the Preston Road corner stood Yeovil's first hospital, built in 1872, with accommodation for only twelve patients, though this number was later increased to twenty. After 1916, until 1968, it served as a Maternity Home. Its site is now part of the roundabout and roadway. Beyond it, in Ilchester Road, a terrace of houses stood high on the bank, and the story of one of them reads like that of the *Marie Celeste*. Unoccupied for some years before the terrace became due for demolition, owing to those road improvements, it had remained furnished and with a dining table set with an unfinished meal. It is said the occupants had been a young married couple who, one breakfast time, had a fierce and final quarrel, both parties leaving in anger to go their separate ways, abandoning their home. After statutory notice had failed to trace ownership, the whole terrace, like the Maternity Home, disappeared with nothing now to show where it had been.

12

'GROVECOTE', PRESTON ROAD.

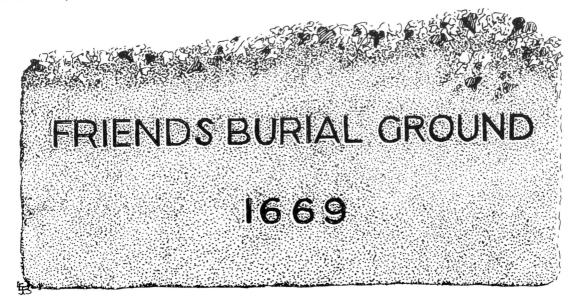

FRIENDS BURIAL GROUND

1669

THE FIVEWAYS HOSPITAL

FORMER TERRACE OF SIX HOUSES NEXT TO MATERNITY HOME, ILCHESTER ROAD

HOLLANDS, ILCHESTER ROAD

On the opposite side of the road, Hollands, a Regency building, is now dwarfed by Yeovil College and used by the Careers Officer, with a chapel in the cellars. But for almost a century it had been owned by banking members of the Batten family. Prior to its acquisition for the building of a new Technical College in its grounds, it had been the residence of Stanley Walter Johnson. Hollands got its name from the de Hollands, Earls of Kent, who were lords of Kingston Manor in the 14th century.

Up Ilchester Road, the former junction with Marsh Lane has now been rounded off, but earlier formed an acute angle, giving to it the name of Piked Weech, and Pycit Cross as far back as the reign of Richard the Second. So the name has nothing to do with a witch, despite the colourful inn sign of the Picketty Witch! The wych was that kind of elm tree which was once a landmark here.

Almost opposite the inn, in a garden wall, is a milestone erected by the Turnpike Trust, which unfortunately has lost its metal one-mile plate, and a little farther on, where the road divides, it was the Trust which cut the right-hand one to improve the route as far as Halfway House. Before this, the route was along the present Martock road past Brimsmore crossroads, which was then the western end of Combe Street Lane. The latter was part of an ancient ridgeway, and at its other end is the site of the Saxon Moot for the Hundred of Stone. The elders of the Hundred – a division of the county – held their meetings here around the stone which gave the Hundred its name, and which still remains in the small park which was the gift of a former Mayor, Alderman Earle Tucker.

15

TURNPIKE MILESTONE, COPPIT'S HILL

BRIMSMORE TREE

THE HUNDRED ST[

SITE OF THE SAXON MOOT - HUNDRED STONE

The corner of Combe Street Lane with Mudford Road was where the Hutt Gate tollhouse stood, to be replaced later by an existing building at the entrance to the former Brickyard Lane, now St Michael's Avenue. Back along Mudford Road, a cottage standing end-on to the road, unlike its neighbours, exhibits a shield bearing the arms of Goodford impaling Cholmondeley. Once, this was the only building standing here, in a field called 'Beacon', and had been provided as a dwelling for an estate employee.

On, past the entrance to Goldcroft where a new Grammar School was built in 1938, a bungalow now occupies the spot where formerly were two thatched cottages, Nos 1 and 2, Green Quarry. Not far away, before piped water became available, a well was bored 'a little above the Kingston turnpike gate', into which the well-sinker accidentally dropped his watch. Despite water being pumped at the rate of thirty gallons a minute for eighteen consecutive hours, the water level could not be lowered, and the watch remained lost.

That turnpike gate stretched across the entrances to Kingston and Higher Kingston, the tollhouse being on the corner formed by the latter with Mudford Road. When the Turnpike Trust was abolished in 1875, the tollhouse was taken down and rebuilt a little way along Kingston, where it remained until the dual carriageway and building of the District Hospital necessitated its removal.

TOLL HOUSE, MUDFORD ROAD

ARMS OF GOODFORD FAMILY, MUDFORD ROAD

NOS. 1 & 2 GREEN QUARRY, MUDFORD ROAD, JUST BEFORE DEMOLITION IN 1958.

UILT KINGSTON TOLLHOUSE

KINGSTON (FIVEWAYS) TURNPIKE GATES AND TOLLHOUSE, c. 1860, from an old photograph.   19

FORMER R.D.C. OFFICES, KINGSTON.

HIGHER KINGSTON FROM FIVE CROSSWAYS c1965.

EOVIL COUNTY SCHOOL' (c1890) LATER TECHNICAL INSTITUTE AND SCHOOL OF ART, KINGSTON. From an engraving.

Also demolished at the same time were premises on the south-western side of Higher Kingston, and the whole of the north-eastern side of Kingston, including Rural District Council offices opposite Kingston House, which is part of the Park School. The terrace of houses adjoining the latter still exhibits, beside each doorway, a reminder of those days when only principal roads were metalled or footpaths paved, when it was frequently necessary to remove mud from one's footwear before entering the house. There are still a few of these bootscrapers to be seen beside shops and dwellings in the town centre.

Another well, sunk by the town council in 1857, to a depth of between 150 and 200 feet, was opposite the Duke of York inn (now Buddy's), while in 1850 there had been a spring known as 'The Fountain' on the site of the County School. The latter became a Technical and Art School when Yeovil School was built in Mudford Road.

Just beyond was the Red Lion Inn and a convenient 'bus stop. Red Lion Lane, giving access to Higher Kingston, separated the inn from Bide's Gardens, originally part of the grounds of Kingston Manor House. Lost when Reckleford was extended through them in 1966, they had been leased to the Corporation as a public park, following acquisition of the manor house and grounds in 1916 for the erection of a General Hospital to replace the, by then inadequate, Fiveways establishment. The manor house became a nursing home attached to the new hospital.

Where the hospital boiler house now stands there was once an ancient chapel of the manor but, by the beginning of the century, the site had become one of Yeovil's many glove factories. The drawing shows it shortly before demolition, when it was the property of Hawkins, Jesty, and Ricketts, while the garden on the right was part of the grounds of Convamore, administrative offices for the hospital.

21

THE RED LION HOTEL, KINGSTON

YEOVIL HOSPITAL FROM BIDE'S
GARDENS, c 1930.

KINGSTON MANOR HOUSE

23

A HIGHER KINGSTON GLOVE FACTORY

Adjoining, the Roman Catholic Church of the Holy Ghost, together with plans for The Avenue, was to the design of Canon A.J.C. Scoles, a former architect. Appointed parish priest in 1878, he purchased some seven acres of land from Captain Prowse, the lord of Kingston Manor, on which to build the church and presbytery. Following the dedication of the church in 1899, Canon Scoles placed the 13th century head of the churchyard cross, which had been discovered in 1853, on the shaft at the entrance to the church. It had been incorporated in The Chantry adjoining the tower of St John's Church, and was found only when that building was rebuilt. Having shown signs of weathering, a replica was made in 1976, and the original placed inside the church.

Before its extension, Reckleford ended here, but a steep descent past a terrace of houses led to the cinema and Court Ash, now marked by a flight of steps. Originally built as the Odeon Cinema, the Cannon occupies the site of Court Ash House, while the cattle market, now a car park but earlier the Fair Ground, was sandwiched between Court Ash and North Lane. At one time a rope walk is said to have extended almost the entire length of the latter, which was also known as Sheep Lane. At the top is the Mansion House, built in the 18th century by banker John Hutchings. James Morse ran a boarding and day school in it for many years in the 19th century. Subsequently the residence of Mayor Sidney Watts, it was offered by him to the Town Council as a mayoral residence, but was refused on the grounds of expense.

24

13c HEAD OF ST. JOHN'S CHURCHYARD CROSS, NOW IN ROMAN CATHOLIC CHURCH OF THE HOLY GHOST, YEOVIL.

ROMAN CATHOLIC CHURCH OF THE HOLY GHOST.

25

NAG'S HEAD AND HOUSES, TOP OF RECKLEFORD

26

COURT ASH and CATTLE MARKET, 1889

MANSION HOUSE FROM NORTH LANE

MANSION HOUSE, PRINCES STREET, 1971.

Park Road, once called Pitney Lane, with Pitney Garden on the corner, divided Hendford from Kingston on that side of Princes Street and, a little way up, on the right, was Hill and Boll's carriage works. Mrs Sophia Hill carried on the business after her husband's death, being described as 'sole proprietor' in 1882. By 1893, John Heinrich Boll had become partner. He came to Yeovil as an apprentice to John Hill, and married Bessie, his employer's daughter, in 1885. A German by birth, he served as an alderman on the Town Council for fourteen years.

The Armoury, now a public house, was the arms repository of the 16th (Yeovil) Rifle Volunteer Corps, whose officers in 1859 consisted of a Captain, Lieutenant and Ensign – the establishment allowed for a corps of sixty. About 1870, it was occupied by drill instructor Symes, and for many years was the sole building on that side of the road.

Then, in 1889, a little farther along, the Reformed Episcopal Church was dedicated as Christ Church, with Rev N. Reader as its minister. Dwindling membership led to its closure after only twenty-four years, its demolition providing materials for the building of Christchurch Villas. These, too, disappeared with the construction of Queensway, though the church font remains as an ornament in Sidney Gardens.

PARK ROAD PROPERTIES DEMOLISHED FOR ROAD WIDENING

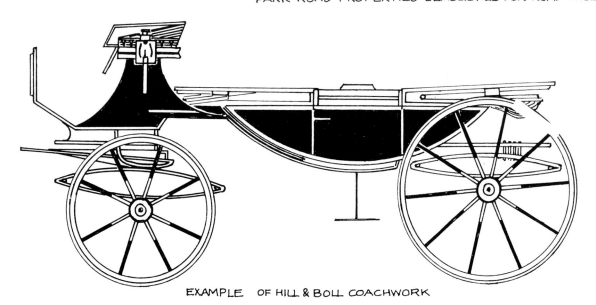

EXAMPLE OF HILL & BOLL COACHWORK

29

EXAMPLE OF HILL & BOLL COACHWORK

THE ARMOURY, PARK ROAD.

CHRIST CHURCH, THE PARK

The making of Queensway was also responsible for the demolition, on the opposite side, of No 16, The Park, which had been the offices of the Area Planning Officer, and next to it, No 18, The Grange had been J.B. Petter's home, then that of J.W. Childs, a builder, and finally the offices of both Weights and Measures and Probation Officers.

On the corner of Clarence Street stands the former Telephone Exchange, bearing a great rarity – the cipher of King Edward VIII. Half way along the street is an unpretentious building, used by John Aldridge for his school – the predecessor of Kingston County School. Its upper rooms were afterwards for some time the Brethren's meeting place.

Back at the bottom of Park Road, the large house on the corner is Old Sarum House, built about 1730 by Samuel Dampier, a wealthy clothier of the well-known East Coker family. His grand-daughter, Susannah, who married John Ryall, a glove manufacturer, inherited the house from her father, another Samuel, about 1778. Eventually the house became the property of John Ryall Mayo, Yeovil's first Mayor. Col William Marsh, a solicitor, later took possession, and it was after his death in 1920 that Yeovil Electric Light and Power Company ruined its appearance by inserting a totally inappropriate shop front on the ground floor. The present accountant occupiers have, at least, presented it with a more dignified appearance.

No.16 THE PARK - OFFICES OF AREA PLANNING OFFICER.

A RARITY - EDWARD VIII DATESTONE
FORMER TELEPHONE EXCHANGE
CLARENCE STREET.

NO. 18 THE PARK. FORMER RESIDENCE OF JAMES B. PETTER

The principal doorway into Glenthorne House used to be that on the south side and, though a canopy above the door has been removed, a delightful lantern fanlight has been retained. The Regency-style west front, however, has been marred on two counts: first, by the removal of glazing bars from the windows, thereby spoiling the symmetry of their appearance and second, by the insertion of a block-like new entrance where there had been a window before, which is totally unsympathetic to the architectural style of the building. However, on the opposite side of the road, the doorway of No 45, giving entrance to dental surgeries on the first floor, is a fortunate and pleasing survival.

Back across the road again, the present entrance to the Conservative Club previously led to Assembly Rooms at the rear, while the Club occupied that part of the premises now the shop of Fox & Co. Whitby's 1904 *Almanack* stated that there was seating for 700, and there were three large dressing rooms. Terms for hiring in 1912 were three guineas for a single night, reducing to 1½ guineas for each of three nights. Many will recall with pleasure the Roc Players repertory company which provided regular entertainment here, with a resident cast including, among others, Michael Goodwin, Frank Middlemass and Ivor Salter. The shop next door in the drawing was that of F. Jenner, bootmaker.

CLARENCE STREET PREMISES WHERE YEOVIL SCHOOL STARTED

OLD SARUM HOUSE, PRINCES STREET

35

LANTERN FAN-LIGHT, GLENTHORNE HOUSE, PRINCES STREET

DOORWAY TO NO.45 PRINCES STREET

GLENTHORNE HOUSE, PRINCES STREET, 1975.

36

CONSTITUTIONAL CLUB AND ENTRANCE TO ASSEMBLY ROOMS, c1900.

Crossing the road yet again, Whitby's bookshop, less familiarly known as Albion House, occupied premises now those of the Halifax Building Society, while a little farther on, where the building line alters, a rainwater head of 1714 shows the initials of John Old and, above it, in the gable end, is a 17th century blocked-up window; note, too, that the tiles are of stone. In 1676, John Old had been a church-warden and, in the year of the rainwater head, agreed to pay the vicar two shillings yearly for an underground drain through the churchyard from his cellar.

On the corner of Church Street until recently, the butcher's shop displayed glazed tiles with the initials 'W & R F Ltd' for Fletchers', previous occupants. There will also be many who recall the little sweet shop, owned by Trevor Parry, which for many years stayed open until 8 o'clock nightly, in order to cater for trade from those attending the adjoining Central Cinema. Built in 1931 to replace the Central Auction Rooms, in which films had been shown previously but which had been destroyed by fire, it was in a style already out of fashion. Both shop and cinema have been replaced by a modern office block.

The early 18th century Church House is one of the town's most attractive buildings, which lost a wing during the 1939–45 war in the course of a bombing raid. Almost certainly built as a town residence by a member of the Batten family, it was later used as their solicitors' offices, still Batten & Co today. On the opposite corner, the former St John's Schoolrooms have been converted into shops on the ground floor, though a little way along Church Path a stone panel records the date of the original construction. Next is The Chantry, removed from the churchyard in 1854. It had once been a chantry chapel which was converted into Yeovil's first grammar school as far back as 1573.

Church Terrace, on the northern boundary of the churchyard, once pleasant private dwellings, has since been converted to office use, and in the process has lost much of its previous charm. But across the churchyard, St John's Church appears very much as it did six centuries ago – a prime example of the early Perpendicular style of architecture. Although the exterior remains largely unaltered in appearance, there have been many changes inside, particularly during the last century. Major restoration of the interior commenced in 1860, when box pews and unsightly galleries were removed, while the provision of the Preston Road Cemetery eventually led to the removal of almost all memorials from the churchyard, and the laying out of colourful flower beds, which now provide such a delightful foreground to Yeovil's oldest building.

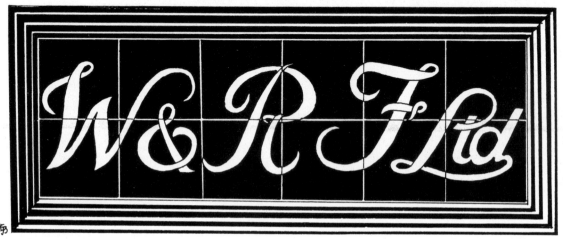

W. & R. FLETCHER MONOGRAPH IN TILES, CHURCH STREET (NOW REMOVED).

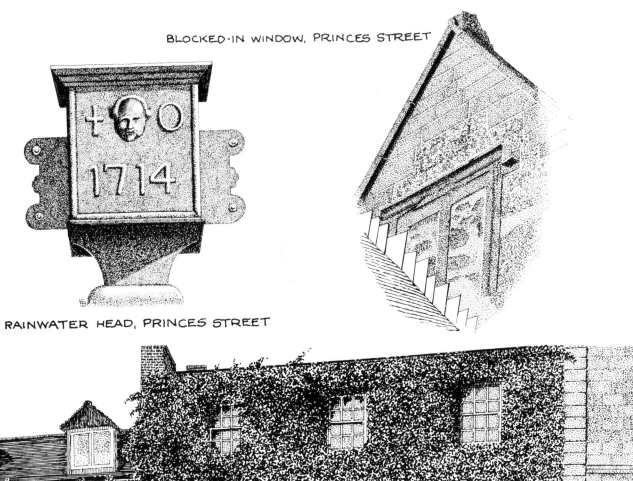

BLOCKED·IN WINDOW, PRINCES STREET

RAINWATER HEAD, PRINCES STREET

WHITBY & SON'S BOOKSHOP, PRINCES STREET

ALBION HOUSE   WHITBY AND SON   STATIONERY OFFICE

BOOKSELLERS   STATIONERS   PRINTERS   LISHERS

SWEET SHOP, CHURCH STREET, 1974.

ORNAMENTAL DETAIL, CENTRAL CINEMA

CENTRAL CINEMA, CHURCH STREET.

41

CHURCH TERRACE

42

STONE PANEL OVER ENTRANCE TO ST JOHN'S
SCHOOLROOMS FROM CHURCHYARD

CHURCH HOUSE, CHURCH STREET

43

THE CHANTRY, CHURCH PATH

During the 19th century, relations were somewhat strained between vicar and organist. When Rev Edmund Wyndham became incumbent in 1873, it was evident he did not see eye to eye with the organist of thirty years' standing, and it was only after protracted and frequently acrimonious disputes that the matter was settled to the organist's satisfaction; he then resigned! But worse was to follow between the next vicar and *his* organist. This time trouble arose over Rev Henry Beebe's wish to introduce a new chant which the organist considered unsuitable; on a Sunday he played the usual accompaniment for the *Te Deum*, but the choir had been instructed to use the vicar's alternative, so 'utter chaos' resulted.

The church suffered some modern damage — bomb blast during the raids of the Second World War necessitated the removal of thirteen windows for repair.

ST. JOHN THE BAPTIST PARISH CHURCH

WEATHERVANE, ST. JOHN'S CHURCH

46

PRIEST'S DOOR, ST. JOHN'S CHURCH, YEOVIL.

GARGOYLE, ST. JOHN'S CHURCH

CORBEL HEADS IN CHANCEL, ST. JOHN'S CHURCH

DECORATIVE DETAIL, PRINCES STREET

CAST·IRON BOLLARD
WATERLOO LANE

UNITED REFORMED CHURCH, PRINCES STREET

Back in Princes Street, the United Reformed Church started as a Congregational Church erected behind the present building in 1792, with its entrance in Clarence Street. The present church, with its pleasing facade at the end of a paved approach, was built in 1878. A little farther on, three decorative heads still adorn shop fronts at about eye level, though generally passed unnoticed while, above the modern offices of the Birmingham and Midshires Building Society, a 'Venetian' window, which should look like the drawing here, is another example of appearance being marred by the removal of glazing bars, and gilt lettering being applied to the inserted pane of glass.

The Westminster Street of today replaced a narrow 'Porter's Lane' which previously led to 'Huish Field', as it was called as late as 1842, and which had been part of Hendford's Saxon open-field system of cultivation. At the top of Waterloo Lane, where Huish starts, a cast-iron bollard still bears the name of the iron-founders, Petter & Edgar.

Yeovil's ageing Swimming Pool, erected in 1884, is due for replacement by a new Leisure Centre elsewhere. On the opposite side of the road, in 1846 the provision of a National School for the education of children of poor parents 'in the principles of the Church of England', was the first of its kind in this area.

SWIMMING POOL, HUISH

'VENETIAN' WINDOW, PRINCES STREET (Restored).

SWIMMING POOL

HUISH NATIONAL SCHOOL, 1845. *From a lithograph*

'THE SALTHOUSE', SALTHOUSE LANE

YEOVIL'S FIRST RAILWAY STATION – AT HENDFORD.   After a lithograph by H.M.Custard.

At the top of Salthouse Lane stood the building where meat was steeped in brine before the days of refrigeration and, at the other end of the lane, was a tan-yard on the corner with West Hendford. The latter had been the original Horsey Lane, as well as that short section bearing the name today. West Hendford was extended beyond this point (where there had been a 'Catchpool' for collecting sewage) along the course of a former footpath, in order to connect with Yeovil's first railway station, linking the town with the main Bristol and Exeter Railway at Durston. Opened on 1 October 1853, the line was closed on 29 May 1968, a victim of the 'Beeching Axe'.

Hendford Lodge, on the corner of Horsey Lane and Hendford, was demolished in 1973 for the construction of the Divisional Police Headquarters, the layout of Queensway, and the Hendford Roundabout. The Volunteer Tavern on the corner of Brunswick Street became a casualty then too. The 17th century portion of Hendford Lodge was incorporated into a larger dwelling towards the end of the 18th century, by a member of the Cayme family of glovers and sailcloth manufacturers. It was subsequently acquired by Robert Tucker, mayor in 1858 and 1859, who was also a glove manufacturer, and who died in the house in 1867.

51

HENDFORD LODGE, NORTH·WEST FRONT

Removal of a number of Hendford properties at about the same time included the pleasant terrace adjoining the entrance to Chant's Path, which had been the original Addlewell Lane – Chant was a builder, living here in the 1840s. The path named after him had been superseded when Brunswick Street was made; part of its course can still be traced along the paved way at the foot of the grass slope at the rear of the Octagon Theatre .

On the opposite side of the road, the initials 'J R M' in a garden wall stand for John Ryall Mayo, first mayor of the Borough in 1854, resident here before inheriting Old Sarum House. Homeville flats occupy the site of a number of quite old houses; the one set back from its neighbours had for some years been St John's vicarage.

Just around the corner, in Manor Road, the shop front of Raymond Bros, notable Yeovil woodcarvers, displays grotesque faces, one of which is drawn here. For a couple of decades at least, at the end of the last century, Tompsett's establishment in West Hendford was cause for complaint from residents in the whole of this area, about 'the abominable stench' caused by his melting of tallow for candle-making.

52

DIVISIONAL POLICE HEADQUARTERS, HORSEY LANE

53

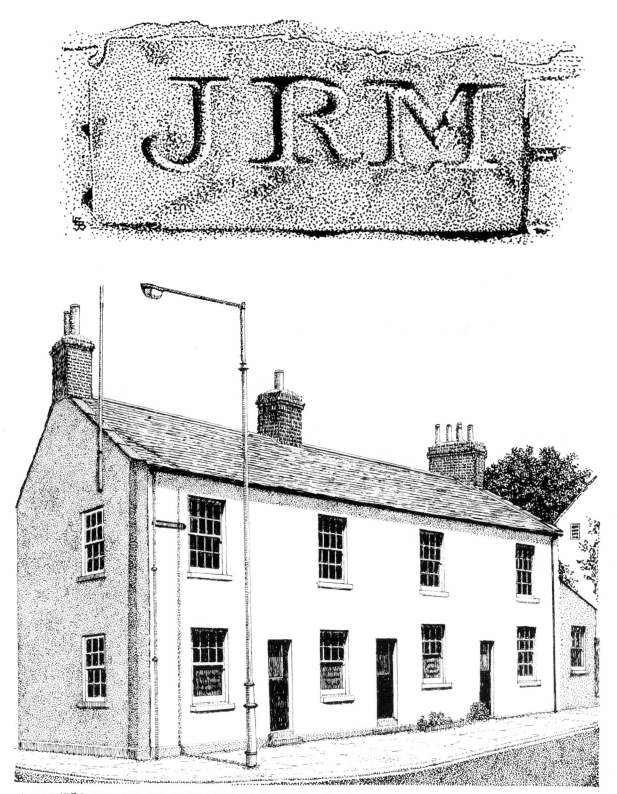

VOLUNTEER INN, CORNER OF BRUNSWICK STREET AND HENDFORD.

ENTRANCE TO CHANT'S PATH FROM HENDFORD

Hendford Manor House, of the mid-18th century, was bought by Yeovil Borough Council in 1936 for £10,000, with the intention of demolishing it in order to create a civic centre in its extensive grounds. Opposition to the scheme at the time resulted in postponement and, during the war, it was occupied in part by Civil Defence Units. Afterwards it was used by several voluntary organisations and the Department of Social Security. Demolition was again proposed in 1975 and a long battle ensued to save the building. But it was not until 1986 that, finally restored, it reopened as six 'luxury' suites of offices.

CARVED HEAD, RAYMOND BROS.

OLD PROPERTIES, HENDFORD, 1965.

56

Behind the building and to one side, the Manor's former coach-house, with its elegant south front, contains the former Borough Council's Wyndham Museum for Yeovil, now redesignated the Museum of South Somerset.

In 1776, John Daniell built Hendford House, now the Manor Hotel, which later became the home of John and Frederick Greenham, glove manufacturers and quarry owners. John Daniell subsequently became a merchant banker, with premises known as Yeovil Old Bank in Hendford, near his house.

Early 19th century Flower's House, once the residence of a well-known Yeovil medical practitioner of that name, still retains on the door-frame his night bell with speaking tube. Earlier, for a number of years, it housed Monk's School, with accommodation for twenty boarders and with a large playground at the rear.

The signboard of the Butchers' Arms inn displays the arms of the Worshipful Company of Butchers, being two poleaxes between bulls' heads, and in chief a boar's head between two bunches of 'holly' – actually 'knee holly', or 'Butcher's broom' – the shoots of this plant were once sold, bundled together, for butchers to sweep their chopping blocks. The building beyond in the drawing, occupied then by Moffat Marine, was later used as a WI Market but, because of its unsafe condition, has recently been demolished.

Hendford Manor, Yeovil

COACH HOUSE OF HENDFORD MANOR

MUSEUM PUMP

MANOR HOTEL, HENDFORD

FLOWER'S HOUSE, HENDFORD

ARMS OF THE WORSHIPFUL COMPANY OF BUTCHERS

BELL AND SPEAKING TUBE –
FLOWER'S HOUSE

BUTCHERS' ARMS AND MOFFAT MARINE, HENDFORD

CHUDLEIGH'S SEED STORE, CORNER OF SOUTH STREET AND HENDFORD

Next again was Chudleigh's Seed Stores, pulled down to improve visibility from South Street. Opposite was the Three Choughs ostler's house, backing on to the hotel's stabling. One of the principal coaching inns, it was formerly owned by the feoffees of Woborn's Almshouse. The inn may have taken its name from the arms of Thomas á Becket, being three choughs, and a play on his name, for a colloquial word for that bird was 'becket'. Around in South Street, above a rear entrance, is a datestone of 1724, with the initial 'G M B'.

Around the corner from the ostler's house, the Oxford Inn stood at the foot of Waterloo Lane. There had been a proposal to turn it into a Watch House and residence for the Superintendent by the Town Commissioners in 1845, but this did not materialise. For some years the offices of a firm of architects, it was eventually demolished.

There are many who will remember when the Cottage Café occupied the present offices of Humberts Estate Agents, but fewer, perhaps, when it was possible to order a joint, two vegetables, with a sweet to follow, for one shilling and sixpence (7½p.). Together with Model Kits, these most attractive premises are almost certainly of 17th century date.

One of the few decorative coal-hole covers now surviving in the town is the one in the pavement opposite Denners in Hendford and, standing on it and looking high above shop window level, one can discern a bearded stone face – an early proprietor? Just around in High Street, the shop-front in the drawing clearly has been retained almost unaltered above ground floor level. It had been built by Edwards & Dean, drapers, in 1836, and acquired by Lindsay Denner in 1895. No 1 Hendford, adjoining, was then Dobell's jeweller's and clock-maker's shop.

THREE CHOUGHS DATESTONE, SOUTH STREET

THREE CHOUGHS OSTLER'S COTTAGE, HENDFORD

63

COALHOLE COVER, HENDFORD

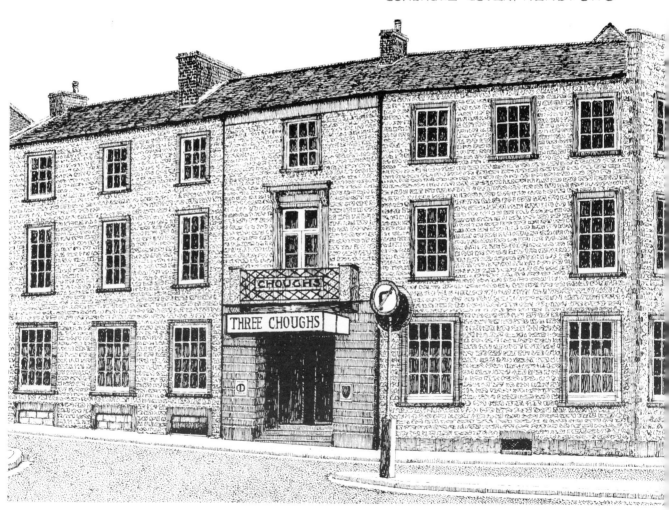

THREE CHOUGHS HOTEL, HENDFORD

64

DENNERS' HEAD

FORMER OXFORD INN ON CORNER OF WATERLOO LANE AND WEST HENDFORD, 1965.

COTTAGE CAFE, HENDFORD.

In the middle of the road, where Princes Street, High Street, and Hendford meet, was a fine three-bracket Sugg gas lamp, a present to the town from the gas company, marking Queen Victoria's jubilee in 1887, at a time when electricity was already beginning to be used for street lighting elsewhere. A similar lamp later appeared in The Triangle. The shop shown in the drawing was replaced soon afterwards by the Capital and Counties Bank, which proudly displayed its armorial bearings right at the top of its corner facade, where they still remain.

The Mermaid, which can claim to be the oldest established licensed premises still in the town, is said to have been in existence here in 1517; certainly it was called 'The Miremaide' in 1629. Like the Choughs, this was well-known as a coaching inn and, when the railway came, a horse omnibus was despatched to meet all incoming trains.

Even when noticed, the entwined initials 'DB' at the top of the building at present occupied by Kitchencraft, opposite King George Street, may convey nothing. But these premises were built as a 'Deposit Bank', Yeovil's first purpose-built savings bank. Now, only pilasters on either side of the shop front remain of its once-elegant appearance.

Fire destroyed the imposing Town Hall on the south side of High Street in 1935. It had been built in 1849 to provide a large meeting-room on the first floor, with accommodation below and at the rear, for much of the business hitherto conducted in The Borough, under a Market House and adjacent Shambles. Buildings stretching to South Street included a meat market, corn exchange, and a cheese and bacon room with flax room over.

CAPITAL AND COUNTIES BANK EMBLEM

L DENNER.

WHITE
UNDERTAKER

DOBELL

RNER OF HIGH STREET AND HENDFORD c1895

67

CORNER OF HIGH STREET AND PRINCES STREET, c1890

68

MONOGRAM OF DEPOSIT (SAVINGS) BANK

MERMAID HOTEL, HIGH STREET

YEOVIL TOWN HALL, HIGH STREET,
1849 - 1935.

70

THE CORN EXCHANGE, REAR OF TOWN HALL.

Of the partners of Denner & Stiby ironmongers' business, next to the Town Hall, Henry Stiby became mayor in 1904, while Thomas Denner was noted for his courteous manner. This, though, was sorely tried on one occasion by a lady who proved difficult when trying to choose a wedding present. After much searching, she at least decided that a coal vase, priced at 25s would be appropriate, and offered 20s. Mr Denner opened the door and with a bow, ushered the lady out, saying, 'Madam, we are not gipsies'.

Their shop, which extended over the entrance to George Court, was sold to J.B. Petter in 1892 as a branch of his main business. Later occupied by Llewellyn, a greengrocer and florist, it was then demolished to allow for the construction of new municipal offices and King George Street.

George Court, or George's Court, giving pedestrian access between High Street and South Street, disappeared at the same time, being partly built over by the new council offices.

In order to make the new street flanked by these new offices, it was necessary to remove Borough House, once the residence of Thomas Binford, a portreeve, then of Dr Flower and, after a short period as an hotel, it was purchased by the Town Council for conversion to a council chamber and offices.

The new offices, incorporating a public library and museum, were completed in 1928, and it was not long before the other side provided a neo-classical streetscape, with the completion of a new Post Office, the main portion of which has since become occupied as Barclays Bank.

With an expanding population following the Second World War, Yeovil's library was hard-pressed to cope with demand and, though the museum was moved away from the first floor to give more office space, the problem persisted. Finally, in 1986, plans for a new library were announced, to be built on ground at the rear and to the side of the existing building.

71

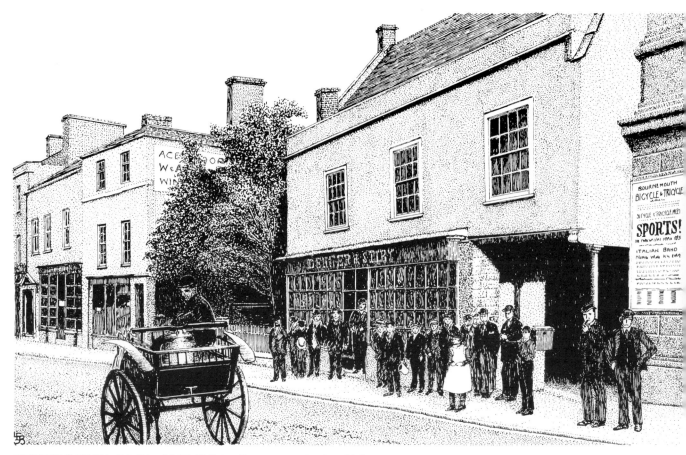

DENNER & STIBY IRONMONGERS' STORE, HIGH STREET, 1883.

DATESTONE OVER ENTRANCE TO FORMER CIVIC BUILDINGS, KING GEORGE STREET

GEORGE COURT LOOKING NORTH TOWARDS HIGH STREET. c1910.

73

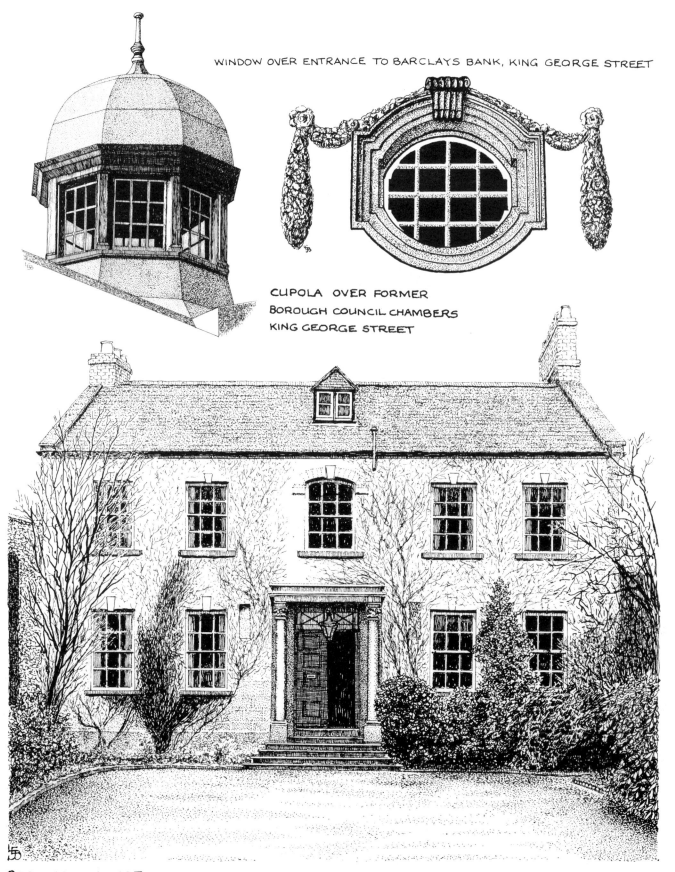

WINDOW OVER ENTRANCE TO BARCLAYS BANK, KING GEORGE STREET

CUPOLA OVER FORMER
BOROUGH COUNCIL CHAMBERS
KING GEORGE STREET

BOROUGH HOUSE

74

BARCLAYS BANK DOORWAY, FORMER POST OFFICE

BARCLAYS BANK DOORWAY, FORMER POST OFFICE

CUPOLA. OF FORMER POST OFFICE
NOW BARCLAYS BANK

SOUTH STREET ~ NORTH SIDE, SITE OF KING GEORGE STREET, PUBLIC LIBRARY, ETC.

Prior to the construction of the street, this had been occupied by several premises, including the former Cheese Market, which had been converted into a fire station in 1913. When these had been removed, the space they occupied off South Street was used to accommodate a children's library and various council employees in 'temporary' wooden huts, with space also for a small car park. It was on this site that the new library was built, and opened in 1987. Excavation work for the foundations revealed a quantity of finds of archaeological interest, recorded by Mr and Mrs B. Gittos, including well sites and, among the artefacts, an almost complete 17th century chamber pot.

South Street, for all of five centuries called 'Back Street', marked the boundary of the medieval borough. No 80, now Yeovil Community Arts Centre, opened in 1988 after many vicissitudes, was for many years a doctors' surgery, though earlier a private residence. The small car park adjoining, where Friday market stalls are set up, was occupied by the residence, and an earlier surgery of Dr Colmer.

Petter's House, opened in 1988, occupies a space which was the end of the garden behind Dr Colmer's house, which was No 79. A footpath beside it led to a large orchard (Yeovil once abounded with orchards) extending over the whole of the area now taken up by the Law Courts, its precincts, and South Street Car Park.

The pre-war Law Courts, incorporating the Police Station, had been intended as the first stage of a planned civic centre.

By taking down Dr Colmer's house, a road was constructed to give access to it. As a second stage, Maltravers House was opened in 1969, housing Government and County Council offices, and it was only then that the road became Petter's Way – previously the Law Courts and Police Headquarters were described as being 'off South Street'.

YEOVIL FIRE STATION, SOUTH STREET, 1913-1962.

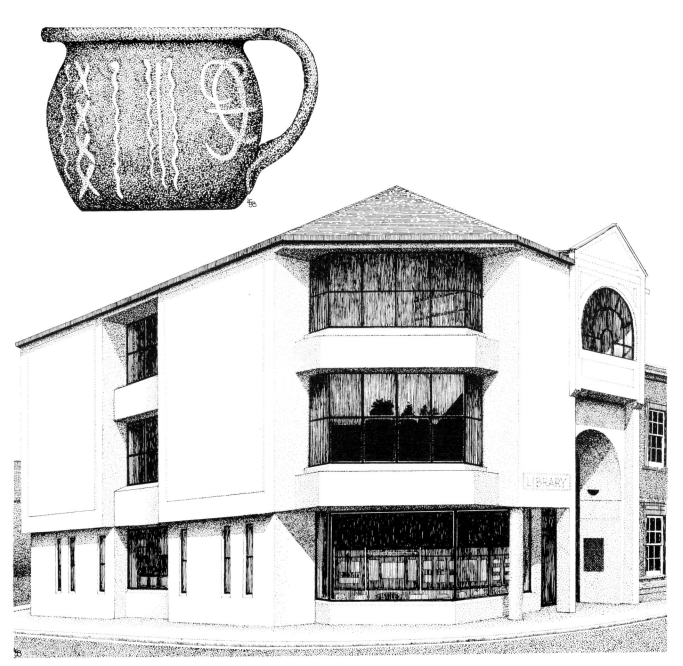

YEOVIL PUBLIC LIBRARY FROM SOUTH STREET

NO. 80 SOUTH STREET

DR. P. A. COLMER'S HOUSE AND SURGERY, 79 SOUTH STREET

PETTER'S HOUSE, PETTER'S WAY

LAW COURTS, PETTER'S WAY

JOHNSON HALL (NOW THE OCTAGON THEATRE), HENDFORD.

MALTRAVERS HOUSE FROM PATH TO PENN PARK

Further development in the area took place with the opening of Johnson Hall in 1974. Built as a multi-purpose civic hall with retractable seating, this has now been re-seated to become the Octagon Theatre.

Back at the entrance to Petter's Way, the Baptist Chapel is built on the site of a barn which was used as a meeting house as far back as 1668. A chapel followed there in 1810, to be replaced by a larger building in 1828. Subsequently enlarged, with a new front and other extensions, it is now again about to be rebuilt, but retaining the frontages of both the church and the adjoining Newnam Memorial Hall, which was erected in 1912.

High on the hill above South Street is the late 18th century Penn House, owned by Peter Daniell (1764–1834), a wealthy mercer and town developer. At the beginning of the 19th century this was the only house standing on the hill, and it was not until some thirty years on, that development commenced with the laying out of Park Street.

It was in this latter street that a great number of workers employed in the glove industry took up residence, and it became noted for the number of public houses it once contained – the Cross Keys, Dolphin, Globe, Golden Lion, Rifleman's Arms and Swan. The last-named was bought by Yeovil Dramatic Society in 1976 and converted into a theatre, which was built on at the rear in 1975 with seating for 144. Since there is a bar adjoining the foyer, in part of the old pub, it can claim to be the only surviving licensed premises in that street.

Emerging from the Swan, the view facing the theatregoer is of the hill which provides such a splendid natural backdrop to the town. To the right, amid the trees, is the famed beauty-spot of Ninesprings. Once available to the public only by ticket obtainable from the owner, Town Clerk Col H.B. Batten, it was eventually acquired by the District Council. The once picturesque thatched cottage where teas were available had suffered neglect during the war years and was allowed to fall into ruin; it disappeared completely. But the area is still a nature-lover's haunt, has recovered much of its former charm, and one can still discover the nine springs which give it its name.

Returning to South Street where once, on the corner, stood the Globe inn and several old cottages, one is opposite Bond Street, which too was only being completed in the 1830s, and where, in 1860, Woborn Almshouse was moved to its new home from medieval buildings in Silver Street. One survival from those previous premises is the large bell, still to be seen at the rear, and which was rung to summon the almspeople to prayers in the chapel. Before turning into Peter Street, notice on the east No 8A, Bond Street, where one of the original round-headed stone door-frames survives alone among the many erected when the street was first made.

In Peter Street, practically all the north side houses have gone to provide a car park and access to the rear of Middle Street stores; where a parking-ticket machine now stands once, for a few months, novelist Thomas Hardy took up residence in the terrace which then existed there. However, in front of one of the two remaining houses, a square coal-hole cover still survives. The street takes its name from Peter Daniell of Penn House, who owned a town house where W.H. Smith's premises are, and whose grounds extended along this street. On the south side, in 1846, Holy Trinity Church was built for the newly-created Hendford Parish, in order to relieve gross overcrowding in the Parish Church of St John the Baptist. The consecration of the new church was celebrated by almost all the town as a public holiday, and schoolchildren were treated to a splendid tea with unlimited plum cake.

BAPTIST CHURCH, SOUTH STREET

PENN HOUSE

SWAN INN, PARK STREET, BEFORE CONVERSION INTO THEATRE

NINESPRINGS

85

GLOBE INN AND ADJOINING COTTAGES, PARK STREET AND SOUTH STREET.

WOBORN ALMSHOUSE, BOND STREET

86

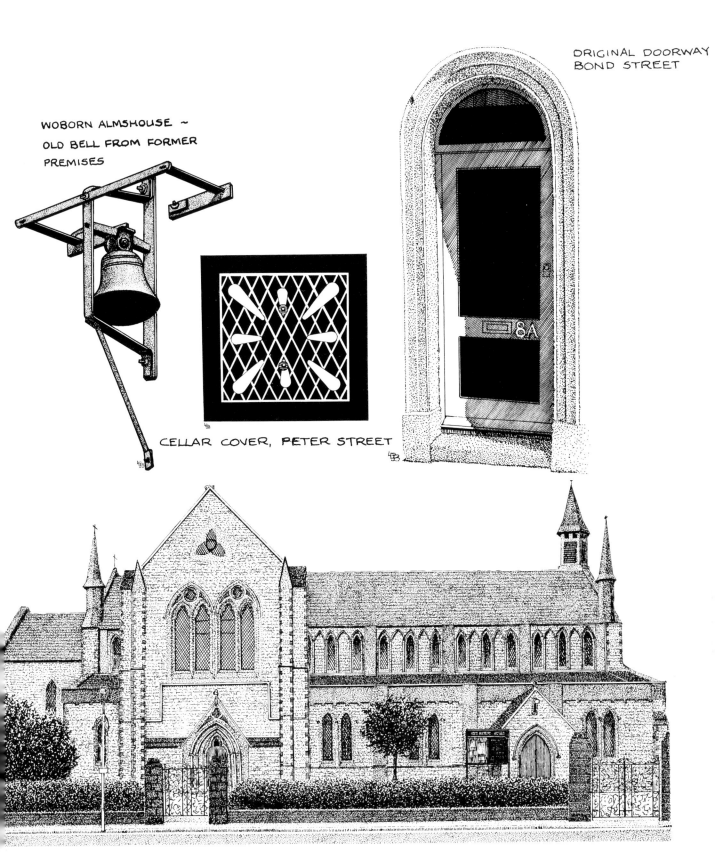

WOBORN ALMSHOUSE ~
OLD BELL FROM FORMER
PREMISES

ORIGINAL DOORWAY
BOND STREET

CELLAR COVER, PETER STREET

HOLY TRINITY CHURCH

In Union Street, the Town House, built by the Town Commissioners in 1849 to house their Surveyor-Superintendent and a Police Station, has just been renovated to become the Mayor's Parlour and Headquarters of Yeovil Town Council. When built, it contained three cells for prisoners with an exercise yard behind, while two doors, one for the surveyor's residence, and the other the police station, opened directly onto the pavement. Both have now become windows, though the northern one still retains the words 'Police Station' cut into the lintel. On the north face of the building, above the cells and just under the eaves, a bell remains which used to be rung to summon the fire brigade. The building continued to house the police force until the completion of Law Courts in Petter's Way.

The forecourt to the Town House was the space occupied by the Portreeve's Almshouse, until it was destroyed by fire in 1910 and was replaced by Dorcas House in Preston Grove. On the opposite side of the street, the Day Centre started out as the Victoria Temperance Hall in 1887, while exactly opposite Union Street was South Street Church of England Schools for Hendford Parish. Built in 1860, they were removed in 1965.

'TOWN HOUSE', UNION STREET.

ENTRANCE TO FORMER POLICE
STATION, UNION STREET

FIRE BELL ON TOWN HOUSE

JTH STREET CHURCH OF ENGLAND (HOLY TRINITY) SCHOOL,   1862 - 1965

A little beyond Union Street, to the west, is the ancient footway known since the early 1800s as Tabernacle Lane, from the Calvinist chapel built in it. As early as 1368 it was Narrow Lane, by 1739 it was Little Lane, and then, sometimes, Hannam's Lane from the proprietor of the successor to Edwards the ironmonger at its entrance in The Borough.

Until 1863 an ancient shop, known as 'Under Bow', stood at the corner of Wine Street (once Grope Lane). It was here, in 1744, that Londoner Robert Goadby inaugurated the *Western Flying Post*, the second only paper to be published in the present county of Somerset. Just around the corner, the Royal Oak, now renamed the 'Hole in the Wall', is basically a 17th century building.

ENTRANCE TO TABERNACLE LANE   90

BYGONE YEOVIL – UNDER BOW, CORNER OF WINE STREET AND HIGH STREET

'ROYAL OAK' (NOW 'HOLE IN THE WALL'), WINE STREET

Medical Hall, facing The Borough, had been long established with a succession of pharmacists culminating in Boots the Chemists, when it was completely demolished by a Nazi bomb. Although rebuilt after the war Boots, after an interval, moved to larger premises and the chemist connection ceased – at present it is a Wimpy Bar.

The Borough, until the second half of the 19th century, presented a totally different appearance. A contemporary pencil sketch of about 1830 shows the market place taken up almost entirely by a 'Market House' – really a roof on pillars – and butchers' shambles. The remains of an ancient market cross were still under the market house, as were town stocks, shown here from a watercolour of 1810. Last occupant of the stocks was a local resident in 1846, when he suffered restraint for several hours for having been found drunk on a Sunday afternoon.

MEDICAL HALL, THE BOROUGH, c1890

YEOVIL MARKET PLACE c1830. *From a contemporary pencil sketch and a lithograph.*

93

TOWN STOCKS UNDER MARKET HOUSE IN THE BOROUGH. *From a watercolour dated 1810.*

Another detail from the same watercolour shows the premises of ironmonger Edwards, later Hannam's, Petter's and Hill Sawtell's, and now, with a less attractive and altered shopfront, Superdrug. The visible remainder of High Street accords with Daniel Vickery's description, that the houses were chiefly of wood and plaster, covered with thatch, and that some had two or three steps descending to the door.

Lloyds Bank opened as the Wilts and Dorset in 1856, on a site which Vickery says had been occupied by 'a block of low mean dwellings'. An old resident, John Plowman, in 1924 recalled an incident relating to the demolition of one of the buildings, which is worth repeating: 'It was a boot shop with thatched roof, which the contractor decided to *pull* down. For this purpose a chain was placed around the building, to which was tied a long rope extending into Wine Street. Adults and children were invited to take hold of the rope and pull, in all sixty or seventy people. When the "long pull" was in progress, the chain broke, and almost all holding the rope fell to the ground'. John's white duck trousers suffered considerably, he declared, from their contact with the mud. The attempt was abandoned and the shop later dismantled by workmen.

Further improvement of this area was proposed in 1911, to celebrate King George V's coronation. This was to demolish the premises now occupied by de Paula Sports, thus opening a view to St John's Church. The then proprietors, the Misses Turner, required a sum which, when invested, would return them an income similar to that they then received. The council decided it could not afford it, and the opportunity was lost.

94

The upper portion of Silver Street had been known as the Corn Market in the 17th century and later while, much earlier, the whole street was referred to as 'Stairs Hill', because of the 'stairs', or steps, leading to the churchyard. The drawing shows part of the old inn and shops standing on the site now occupied by the Silver Street frontage of Marks and Spencer's store.

On fair days, at the beginning of this century, the street was particularly congested. A newspaper report of 1906 described the scene as 'a pandemonim of shouting "copers", fluttering flags, and plunging horses, and considerable agility was demanded of passers-by to get through the press without damage'.

Lower down, the Pall signboard recalls a pall belonging to Woborn Almshouse, which was kept there for hire. The almshouse was where the Toby Grill of the Tavern now stands. The small courtyard of the tavern, on the corner, was where a larger Horse Pond existed, and where a ducking-stool had once been maintained. When the inn was being rebuilt in 1836, the Town Commissioners ordered it to be set back 'to conform with the rest of the adjoining premises', and the Horse Pond was drained and filled in at the same time. In 1837, the *Victoria* day coach left three times a week from the Pall for Salisbury, the journey taking seven hours.

STREET LOOKING WEST, 1810. *From a watercolour.*

95

Proposed Scheme of 1911, after a drawing by J.N. Johnston.

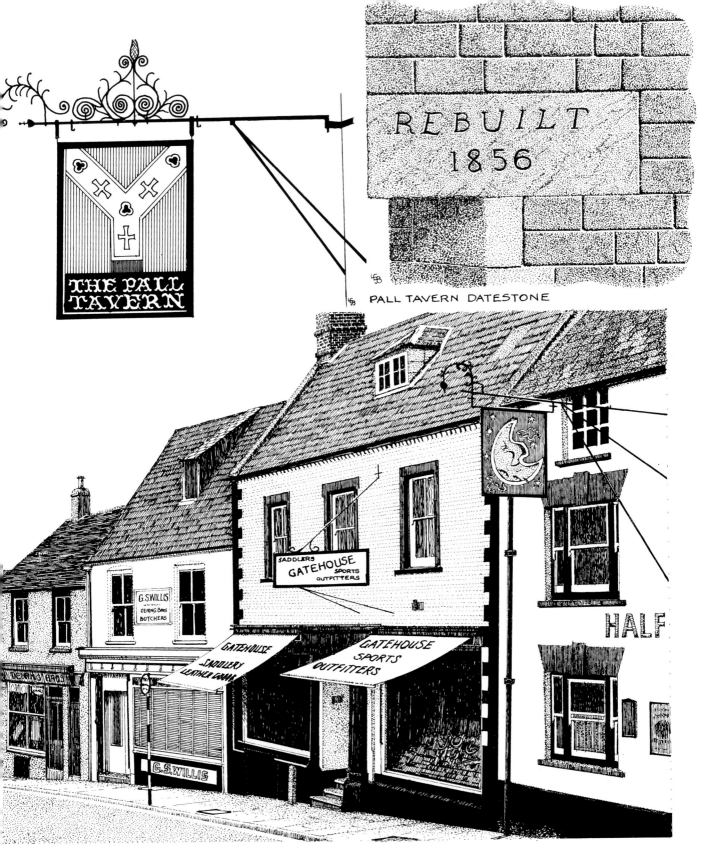

THE PALL TAVERN

REBUILT 1856

PALL TAVERN DATESTONE

SADDLERS
GATEHOUSE SPORTS OUTFITTERS

G.S.WILLIS
DEALING BROS
BUTCHERS

GATEHOUSE
SADDLERY
LEATHER GOODS

GATEHOUSE
SPORTS
OUTFITTERS

G.S.WILLIS

HALF

UPPER SILVER STREET, 1965.

On the corner of Court Ash, opposite, is Palmer Snell's office, formerly a private residence with a pleasing doorway. Immediately behind this building in Market Street was Miller's Well, which had existed there from at least 1367. Until the transfer of the market to Court Ash, Market Street had been the original Reckleford, or 'Rackelford'. The 'Rackel' stream crossed the road at the bottom of Silver Street, causing a shallow ford, feeding the Horse Pond and flowing eastward behind Vicarage Street houses. By the middle of the 19th century it had become nothing more than a sewer.

At the other end of Market Street, its junction with Reckleford Hill, until the construction of the dual carriageway, was called Reckleford Cross, and this was the name also given to the school there run by the Misses Chaffey. In the early part of the 19th century, a wayside cross actually stood in the middle of the road here, and is shown on a map of Yeovil drawn by E. Watts in 1806.

On the far side of the road, not long after the cross was demolished, Reckleford House was built by glove manufacturer William Whitby, who rented it to Thomas Dampier, another glover, who continued to live there until inheriting Kingston Manor. Another of the gloving fraternity, Richard Ewens, acquired it, and his widow continued to live there until after 1920. It was used as offices by the Western Electricity Supply Company in the 1930s and, after the war, the Ministry of National Insurance occupied it from 1948 until the building of Maltravers House in 1969. The house was demolished a short while later.

A row of cottages, typical of other glove-workers' dwellings further along the road, now completely vanished, ran to the corner of Goldcroft. It was in the latter road in 1925 that the two 'Pettren' houses there were erected as prototypes, designed by Yeovil architects Petter & Warren with a roof to the plan of Col Nissen, whose name is perpetuated by military huts. They were intended as a cheap solution to the acute housing shortage following World War I but, although others followed elsewhere, they were not popular, and less economic in construction than had been anticipated. The importance of these Yeovil examples was recognised by the Department of the Environment in 1983, when they were listed as being of special architectural interest.

Back in Reckelford, opposite Goldcroft there was once a rope and twine works where later Salisbury Terrace was built, only to be pulled down for the construction of the dual carriageway. Further along, the Glovers' Arms is a 17th century building, still a farmhouse on the outskirts of the town in 1840. Its signboard displays the arms of the Worshipful Company, to remind us of the once-flourishing industry of which not a single working factory now remains. Across the road at the end of Eastland Road, formerly Kiddle's Lane and even earlier Ryall's Lane, is the building which until now has been the Goldcroft Leather Dressing Factory, formerly Raymond's. Farther up the road is an example of a Victorian terrace whose name, like many another, is now disregarded, except for the reminder of the datestone. The mechanism of the clock standing over Reckleford Junior School once marked the passing of time outside the Town Hall in High Street.

Passing back through the 'Bus Station with its Glovers Walk logo of five-fingered gloves, and ascending the escalator to Ivel Square (another set of the same), Vicarage Walk in the Quedam is on a level above the Vicarage Street of yesteryear. Practically all that remains recognisable of the former street is the Methodist Church, shown here before a bomb destroyed its schoolrooms. It had been built in 1870, where once had been 'some dismal-looking cottages, known as the Old Workhouse, and a house and garden adjoining'. Opposite was the Britannia Inn, whose licensee in the years before the First World War was Job Mitchell who, besides hiring out horses, traps and waggonettes, dealt in turf supply. Since, when burnt on fires, peat is particularly sooty, he was able to deal with this too; he was also a chimney-sweep!

DOORWAY, COURT ASH HOUSE

RECKLEFORD HOUSE

99

COTTAGES FORMERLY IN RECKLEFORD

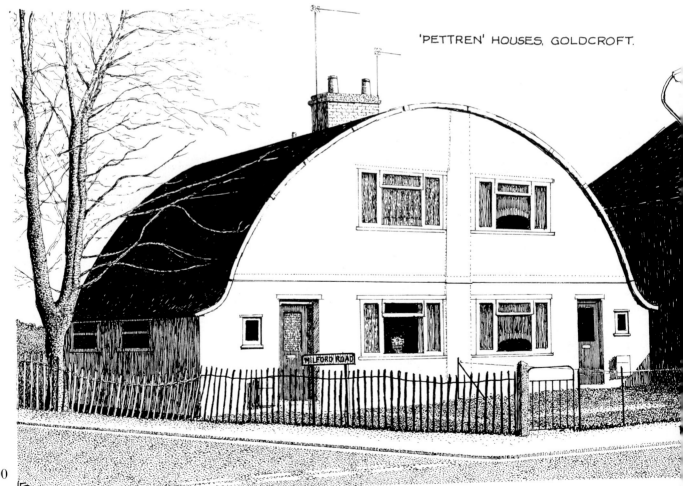

'PETTREN' HOUSES, GOLDCROFT.

ARMS OF THE WORSHIPFUL COMPANY OF GLOVERS

GLOVERS' ARMS, RECKLEFORD

RECKLEFORD JUNIOR SCHOOL CLOCK

LEATHER DRESSING FACTORY, EASTLAND ROAD

VICARAGE STREET METHODIST CHURCH AND SCHOOLROOMS, c 1890.

VICARAGE WALK FROM IVEL SQUARE, THE QUEDAM

THE BRITANNIA INN, VICARAGE STREET

Just around the curve, the premises there were typical of the whole street; like Park Street, this was where a large number of those employed in the leather and glove industries lived. Frederick Place descended steeply from Middle Street a little way along and, just beyond that again, was the Vicarage Street Hall, built in 1818 as Yeovil's first Sunday School by the Portreeve and Burgesses at a cost of £375. Later it became the Brethren's meeting hall.

The vicarage of St John's, which gave the street its name (it had been Quedam Street earlier), occupied the space later taken up in part by Quidham Place. The *Western Flying Post* in 1860 reported that the vicarage had undergone many transformations in the six centuries of its existence, but that in 1856 a few of the original stone doorways still existed and, 'about two years ago, the house was sold to Mr Ensor, glove manufacturer, and another vicarage house was bought in Hendford'.

SOUTH SIDE OF VICARAGE STREET APPROACHING METHODIST CHURCH, 1965

ENTRANCE TO FREDERICK PLACE FROM VICARAGE STREET, 1965

VICARAGE STREET HALL, 1965

QUIDHAM PLACE, VICARAGE STREET, 1931

Towards the western end of Vicarage Street, on the north side, stood the Unitarian Chapel. This had been built on the site of a building once the property of one of the chantries in St John's church, and which had been hired by the evicted vicar, Rev Henry Butler, in 1687. The property was purchased in 1704, and the old meeting house was replaced by a new building in 1809 on the same site. This is the one shown in a plan made in 1892, when substantial alterations were then made. When the Unitarians moved to a hut in Kingston, the chapel was converted into a store by agricultural engineer Percy Winsor, and finally demolished. When the site was being excavated for the Quedam development, a tomb, which had been in the original forecourt of the chapel, was uncovered. This contained a lead-lined coffin believed to hold the remains of Robert Batten.

The western end of Vicarage Street included the building which was the headquarters of Yeovil Volunteer Fire Brigade, from its formation in 1860 until 1913. This triangular building owed its peculiar shape to a fire which had destroyed the premises formerly on the site for, in rebuilding, the street was widened, which shows how narrow the entrance must once have been. In the days of manually-operated fire engines, the brigade issued a token which was given to those who assisted the brigade, redeemed at headquarters the following day, at the rate of one shilling for those who worked at the double-handled pump, while those who helped with the hose received 2s 6d each – leather hoses were notoriously leaky!

FORMER UNITARIAN CHAPEL, VICARAGE STREET, CONVERTED AS STORE FOR PERCY WINSOR

WESTERN END OF VICARAGE STREET, WITH UNITARIAN CHAPEL ON RIGHT

YEOVIL VOLUNTEER FIRE BRIGADE

FIRE ENGINE OPERATIVES' TOKEN

VICARAGE STREET, WESTERN END, 1965.

VICARAGE STREET FIRE BRIGADE BUILDING (1861-1913) IN 1965.

VICARAGE STREET, WESTERN END, 1975.

112

How vastly the scene had changed within ten years is shown by the drawings made in 1965 and 1975, from about the same spot. By the latter date, the opposite side of the street, shown by the drawing from Silver Street, had for some time been a car park – now it is where the Quedam toilets are sited.

At the top of Middle Street a cupola is a striking corner feature of the Midland Bank. Here in the 16th century was a property belonging to a chantry, which became the 'Church House', a medieval social centre. Middle Street then, and for long afterwards, was called 'Pit Lane' because it led to the nether regions (?), or more probably because of tan or flax pits.

Almost opposite Union Street, the gable front of Adams' clothes store displays a carved wooden portcullis at its apex, a reminder that these premises were formerly those of W.H. Smith & Son. The premises they now occupy, exactly opposite, had been Yeovil Post Office from 1902 until 1928. Still to be seen on this building are a lion's head and squirrels, Post Office emblems, the latter promoting National Savings. Until a few years ago, a metal ring could still be seen in the kerbstone outside a Union Street side entrance, once used to tether horses drawing parcels delivery vans.

The Castle Hotel, which stood where Peter Lord's shoe shop is now, had been called the Hart some time before 1680; then, until 1750, it was the Higher Three Cups before being again renamed as The Castle. It, too, had been chantry property and in its heyday was renowned for extensive stabling and the number of horses maintained at the rear of the inn.

VICARAGE STREET ENTRANCE FROM SILVER STREET

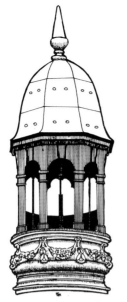

MIDLAND BANK CUPOLA

A MIDDLE STREET PORTCULLIS!

KERB-STONE TETHERING RING

YEOVIL POST OFFICE 1902-1928

CASTLE HOTEL · MIDDLE STREET.

The George, a little lower down on the opposite side – Primark marks its site – had started as a private house, and in 1478 was owned by the trustees of Woborn Almshouse, who continued to hold it until 1920 when it was sold to Lovibonds, the brewers. It had become an inn by 1650 with the name of the Three Cups, which explains the earlier name of the Castle. Three cups, by the way, were the arms of the Worshipful Company of Salters. In the 17th century, the inn had the misfortune to accommodate a traveller suffering from plague, which spread through the town with devastating effect in 1646. This half-timbered building, called the George from at least the early part of the 19th century, was pulled down in 1962, much to the regret of all. It had been the most westerly example of this Wealden type of house.

The entrance to Frederick Place has now been disfigured by a tubular monstrosity indicating the way to The Quedam, but it is still possible to discern the bearded face on the keystone of the original arch. Perhaps this is a portrait of Frederick Cox, to whose builder's yard this once led. It was only after his death that a petition of 1890 resulted in it becoming a right of way. The stone doorcase of the Ivel Club, just beyond the entrance, had weathered too badly to save it for re-erection when it became due for dismantling. Another whimsical head, with wings, is to be seen on the chimney stack above Boots Opticians.

116

IVEL CLUB DOORFRAME, FREDERICK PLACE.

CHIMNEY STACK GROTESQUE

FREDERICK PLACE KEYSTONE

THE GEORGE INN, YEOVIL. Demolished 1962.

The space where Middle Street is joined by Stars Lane, South Street, and what remains of Vicarage Street, has for long been known as 'The Triangle' though, like 'The Borough', it is not officially recognised as such by street name-plates. The area in front of Harris Carpets did, in fact, once form a triangle, with houses destroyed in 1896. In earlier times this was Vennells Cross, from the Latin *venella*, a lane. The lane which separated the triangle from the buildings between Middle Street and South Street was Turnstile Lane, from the barrier in its centre to prevent its use by other than pedestrians, (more popularly known as 'Lollipop Lane' by children, because sweets were obtainable from a grocer's shop there).

The heavy load being drawn by two traction engines in the drawing shows its appearance almost immediately before demolition to build a new Co-operative Society Store, which is the present building. The date 1910 on the centrepiece at the top shows also clasped hands and a wheatsheaf, the latter for long the trademark of own-brand products of the Society. Balancing this datestone, decorative features flank it on either side.

Here was where Middle Street once ended and the Fore Street of medieval times began. When the Triangle buildings were removed, a three-bracket Sugg gas lamp, similar to that in High Street, was erected and, later, underground toilets were provided. On the north side of the street, the Coronation Hotel replaced an earlier Blue Ball Inn and next to the hotel an entrance led to Whitby's large glove factory. Beyond that were a series of three shops under pale green copper domes – Freeman, Hardy & Willis shoe stores, Maynard's sweet shop, and Tom Coombs' cake shop.

An earlier appearance, about 1920, shows the present pedestrian precinct, drawn from a photograph by F.G. Christopher, a noted professional recorder of local scenes, but whose negatives, sadly, were destroyed after his death. This scene, like others, graphically recalls a time when standing or walking in the road did not present the same hazards it would today!

On the right, Jesty's furniture store was later taken over by the Co-op; above it there still existed the former Wesleyan chapel built in 1834. Cottages on a bank level with the chapel on that side of the street were known as Ebenezer Row, since all nonconformist places of worship were known as 'Ebenezers'.

Back on the north side, the whole of the premises there were swept away in redevelopment about 1965, when uniformity was the planners' ideal, and Glovers Walk, with its well-designed logo of gloves above, was made to give access to the small shopping mall and the 'Bus Station beyond. An earlier glove emblem, now removed to the Museum, was the weathervane above the former glove factory at the end of Stars Lane, which is now used by a number of businesses.

There are many handymen who will have used Higdon's ironmonger's business for DIY activities. Its predecessor here was a coachbuilder, whose 'Yeovil Cart' is illustrated. His name aptly reflected his workmanship – Frederick Gracious Style.

It was on about this spot that a bridge once carried the road over the Rackel and Milford Streams, which ran into the 'Withy Bed' opposite. This was drained in 1833, when Yeovil Gas and Coke Company was established, with retorts and gasholders installed on the site. The former offices remain but, as a result of ill-considered alterations, the dignified appearance they once presented is barely distinguishable.

Where 'Living Homes' now occupy corner premises at Central Road, there had been the Railway Tavern, which itself had moved sideways for the construction of that road in 1913. An area at the rear, known as Hoare's Yard (George Hoare was the licensee), was where 'portables', as the acting fraternity referred to travelling performances, were staged. Known as 'Penny Pops' locally, these popular entertainments put in more or less regular appearances every couple of years.

MIDDLE STREET ENTRANCE TO FREDERICK PLACE (PRE-QUEDAM)

119

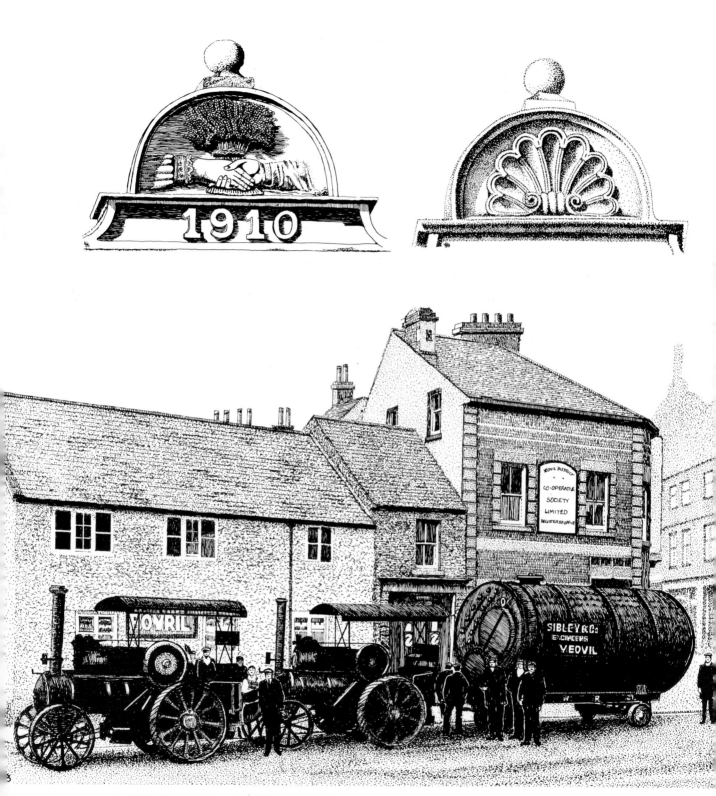

A HEAVY LOAD IN THE TRIANGLE, 1910. *From a photograph dated 23 March 1910.*

'THE TRIANGLE' 1965.

WEATHERVANE FORMERLY ON A GLOVE
FACTORY IN STARS LANE

T. JESTY

LOWER MIDDLE STREET FROM THE TRIANGLE, c.1920.   From a photograph by F. G. Christopher.

REAR OF METHODIST CHAPEL, MIDDLE STREET.

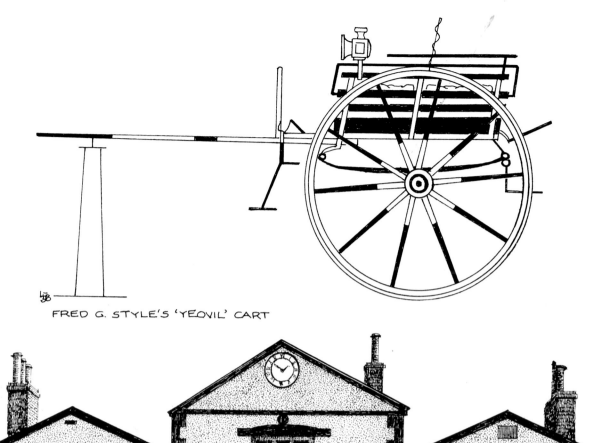

FRED G. STYLE'S 'YEOVIL' CART

ENTRANCE TO GAS WORKS, MIDDLE STREET, c1955.

In 1861 Yeovil Town Railway Station, designed by Sir William Tite, was opened jointly by the London and South Western and the Bristol and Exeter Railway Companies, each with its own stationmaster. Hendford Station was then relegated to the handling of goods. The coming of the railway had the effect, eventually, of almost trebling the growth of the town's trade and population, but piecemeal development by several companies resulted in wasteful arrangements. One central station would have been far more effective in moving traffic, and with a greater economic efficiency. Instead, there were three widely separated ones, particularly that at the Junction. So, when Dr Beeching wielded his 'axe', Yeovil lost its branch line to Taunton, its convenient Town Station, and consequently its shuttle service to and from the main London to Exeter line. All that now remains of the Town Station is a datestone set in the toilet block in the car park it once occupied.

Looking down on that car park from the hill above is the Summerhouse which gives the hill its name. Built by a member of the Harbin family of Newton Surmaville, it is said to have provided a means for signalling communication between them and the Phelips family, at the tower on St Michael's Hill at Montactue.

In Newton Road, on the corner of South Western Terrace, Newton Lodge was the toll house which had replaced an earlier house and gate at Penstile – where the *Western Gazette* offices are at present, on the corner of Sherborne Road.

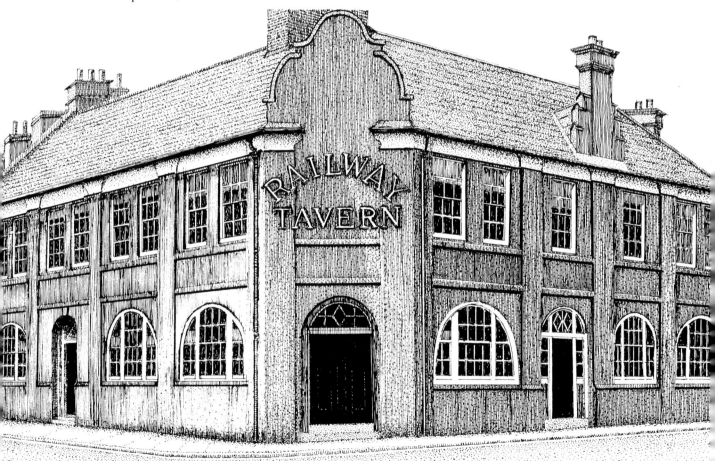

RAILWAY TAVERN, MIDDLE STREET

YEOVIL TOWN RAILWAY STATION

SHUTTLE TRAIN FROM YEOVIL JUNCTION APPROACHING NEWTON ROAD
BRIDGE TO DISEMBARK PASSENGERS AT YEOVIL TOWN STATION, 1965.

THE SUMMERHOUSE, NEWTON HILL.

Before Ivel Court replaced the former Western Counties Creameries factory, the initials 'AB' were prominently cut in stone on the building. J.S. Aplin and W.H. Barrett joined forces to build the factory in 1897; the company then formed included products from Maynards, and from E.D. Marsden. 'St Ivel' cheese first appeared as a brand name in 1901. Bought by Unigate in 1960, the Yeovil factory was closed in 1976 and the St Ivel sign remained for only a short while afterwards.

The adjoining *Western Gazette* offices were built in 1906 to replace their former premises opposite in Newton Road. The head of Mercury which appears over the doorway is a reminder of the paper's origins in the *Sherborne Mercury*, started in 1737.

Opposite, on the corner of Wyndham Street, Clements Corner Store was removed to improve visibility. The firm also had another store in High Street. Wyndham Street had been cut by the Town Commissioners, who obtained land 'in Townsend Close' in 1835 for the purpose.

The rural aspect of this part of Yeovil is shown by the existence of Sun House Farm, where Southville now joins Sherborne Road; until well into the second half of the 19th century, the road was known as the London Road.

At the top of the hill, immediately before Larcombe's Corner, Primrose Terrace exhibits terra-cotta cherubs' heads and a datestone of 1885. The rising ground here is known as Goar Knap, a survival from Saxon times, the first part being the same as *gore* – a tapering shape – which is formed by the Lyde Road junction.

YEOVIL TOWN RAILWAY STATION DATESTONE

APLIN & BARRETT MONOGRAM ON FORMER PREMISES, NEWTON RD.

NEWTON LODGE, FORMER TOLLHOUSE, NEWTON ROAD

FORMER STORES ON CORNER OF WYNDHAM ST. AND SHERBORNE ROAD.

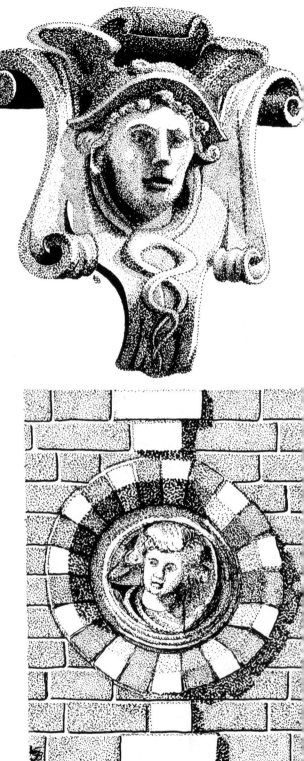

PRIMROSE TERRACE TERRA-COTTA HEAD

STILE, SHERBORNE ROAD, LEADING TO PEN MILL STATION

SUN HOUSE FARM, SHERBORNE ROAD *from a contemporary oil painting.*

FORMER PEN MILL INN · SHERBORNE ROAD

Pen Mill railway bridge, which has one of those narrow types of stile one has to squeeze through, meant the raising of the road to pass over the line. In doing so, the former Pen Mill Inn was left below on the old level and isolated from the new road, and it reverted to private dwellings. They were demolished not long after the opening of Pittard's modern tannery in the ground adjoining.

Chudleigh's Mill continued on the undoubted site of one of two mills recorded for Yeovil in the great Domesday Survey of 1086. This was the mill of Kingston Manor; the other, Frogg Mill at the foot of Mill Lane, has now completely disappeared.

Marking the limit of the former Corporation's jurisdiction, when Yeovil possessed borough status, is one of several attractive signs set up at main road entrances, and which still remain.

Finally, there is the tollhouse, just over Yeo Bridge, re-sited from Goar Knap. The triangular projection enabled the keeper to view the road in both directions, besides providing a convenient place to hang the gate with a bell above, which a coachman could ring to attract the tollkeeper's attention. So our perambulation, which started on the far side of the town, ends here on Dorset soil which, appropriately, was also a gathering point for perambulation of parish boundaries in times past..

132

BOROUGH
OF
YEOVIL

CHUDLEIGH'S MILL, PEN MILL

YEO BRIDGE TOLL HOUSE

INDEX

SUBSCRIBERS

Presentation Copies

1 Yeovil Town Council
2 Yeovil District Council
3 Somerset County Council
4 Yeovil Library
5 The Yeovil Community Arts Centre
6 The Museum of South Somerset
7 Cllr John Cruddas
8 David Young

9 Leslie & Marjorie Brooke
10 Clive & Carolyn Birch
11 K. Jenkins
12 Miss G.M. Symons
13 Mrs A.B. Edwards
14 P.T. Wry
15 Miss Anne Shillabeer
16 Mr & Mrs P. & D. Drayton
17 T.R. Card
18 Gwyn & Isabel Thomas
19 Mrs Patricia Stewart
20 Mr & Mrs P. Hingley
21 Miss J. Harper
22 Yeovil Library
26
27 Crewkerne Library
28 Local History Library, Taunton
29 Mrs P.J.M. Green
30 Miss A.J. Cousins
31 Penelope Thomas
32 J.D. Le Feuvre
33 G.H. Austen
34 Mr & Mrs J. Bottle
35 Mr & Mrs K.J. Bottle
36 Betty Bowstead
37 Mr & Mrs I.C. Leary
38 Mr & Mrs D.C.F. Scammell
39 M.J. Green
40 F.E. Burroughes
41 W.F. Denman
42 Mrs J. Kennedy
43 D. Courage
44 Martyn & Barbara Shire
45 C.A.F. Hawkins
46 D.A. Green
47 Mrs M.E.C. White
48 G.H. Thorne
49 L.J. Dicks

50 Robin Ansell
51 A.J. & G.E. Prosser
52 Harry & Rose Ridgewell
53 S.J. Wills
54
55 B.G. Cripwell
56 Mr & Mrs N.G.P. Kibby
57 J.R. Brookes
58 Miss A.S. Mitchell
59 J.P.O. Lewis
60 R.W.G. Price
61 F. Price
62 Paul & Marion Rose
63 C.R.K. Dore
64 Philip G. Billing
65 Stephen R. Smith
66 Peter J. Baker
67 Theresa & Michael Randall
68 Mrs J.E. Robinson
69 Sheila & Eric Dove
70 Erica & Roger Woolmington
71 Derek Cane
72 Paul Gale
73 Philip Rendell
74 Mrs C. Bryant
75 Mrs D.J. Howard
76 Mrs J.K. Riley
77 Mrs Nina Hayward
78 Allan Rendell
79 Mrs Gladys Trim
80 Syd Wignall
81 Miss E.J. Taylor
82 D.A. Richards
83 R.J. Parsons
84 C.N. Payne
85 Mrs C. Hawkins
86 Michael H.J. Zair

87 Karl Dover
88 J. Lester
89 David Dale
90 Mrs Shillabeer
91 Mr & Mrs D. Puddy
92 E. Morgan
93 Jean Pilgrim
94 F.A. Dare
95 S. Tuck
96 R.F. Boulton
97 D. Ayres
98 D.J. Shears
99 Mrs D. St John Rushton
100 Mrs M. Amor
101 B. Lee
102 Miss E. Ann Swain & Mrs G.F. Dunton
103 D.G.W. Pippard
104 A. Pacey
105 R.J.S. Betts
106 Mrs J.M. Lucas
107 Mr & Mrs P.R.T. Somerset
108 A.R. Chinn
109 R. Jacklin
110 E.C. English
111 E. Ford
112 E. Mason
113 Garry Martin
114 David Kettlety
115 T. Blackburn
116 D.R. Smith
117 C.M. Haine
118 Mrs V.K.M. Hill
119 Angela G. Eason
120 James R. Drayton
121 D.C. Smith
122 Mrs P. Batstone
123 Mrs H.R. Kennett

124 Mrs M.M. Philips
125 P.J. Webber
126 Mrs H. Webber
127 Miss I.D. Reeves
128 E.H.R. Young
129 S.B. Gibbons
130 Charles & Sophia
131 Campbell
132 June E.M. Dawson
133 Jacqueline B.A. Tydeman
134 John Bowes
135 Mrs B.M. Burnett
136 Anthony Masters
137 Miss L.J. Rose
138 Colin T. Hill
139 Miss P.A. Legg
140 Stephen Mogg
141 W.G. Thorn
142 Mrs Jean Templeman
143 G.A. Goldsmith
144 Mrs Ruth Gay
145 Alun Kames
146 Mr & Mrs C.L. Hill
147 Tom Hardisty
148 Bertie Hardisty
149 Jack Hardisty
150 Barrie Wheatley
151 Nick Speakman
152 Miss Elizabeth Gowers
153 M.T. Davies
154 F.N. Taylor
155 J. Jones
156 Chrissie Gee
157 Sheila Holliday
158 Hilda & Geoffrey Gillham
159 Andy Le Fevre
160 Mr & Mrs G.W. Raymond
161 P.R.D. Wilson

162 L.C. Hayward
163 Bunty & John Moon
164 Ronald Dash
165 Gary Peter Hobbs
166 Museum of South
    Somerset
167 Brian & Moira Gittos
168 Muriel Crewe Gittos
169 Tobias Stok
170 Mr & Mrs Nile
171 Dawn & Colin Veale
172 Anthony & Ann Dening
173 Peter & Tracey Brooke
174 David Brooke
175 Jayne Kirk
176 Mrs M.A. Clelland
177 Barbara & Clem
    Shepherd
178 Arthur Malcolm Cooper
179 J.P.A. Smalley
180 Audrey R. Wood
181 Brian Reginald Bartlett
182 Clifford F. Brown
183 Sue & Jeff Sully
184 Mrs I.L. Brice
185 *The Visitor*
186 Jean & Ron Batty
187 Norman & Jean Preston
188 R.A. Beable
189 Mr & Mrs Brian Kibby
190 Ralph Radcliffe
191
192 Terence Peter Farmer
193
194 Nigel Martin
195 Mr & Mrs R.F. Amatt
196 Paul Amatt
197 Mr F.G. & Mrs R.M.
    Alstone
198 Robert John Bond
199 Ernest Colville-North
200 Wilfred E. Perry
201 Miss M.E. Greaves
202 Mrs & Mrs T.H. Quirk
203 David Young RIBA
    MSAI ACIArb FRSA
204 J.F.C. & E.R. Jones
205 Pauline Kibblewhite
206 J.L. Diment
207 R.J. & A. Woodward
208
209 Glenn R. Smillie
210 Alan Davies
211 D.N. Moon
212 Patrick Lintern
213 E.N. Bangay
214 Michael & Nicola Evans
215
216 Miss Janet Lawrence
217 Harold & Clarissa Cargill
218 L.D. Palmer
219 Paul Hillard
220 Pauline Mary Westcott
221 R. Rousell
222 Mrs A.J. Cave
223
224 Mrs H. Cousins
225 Brenda L. Herrin
226 Peter D. Hossent
227 Mrs R.H. Pearce
228 A.J. Gordon
229 Mrs D. Trigg, Librarian,
    Preston School

230 Dennis Buttle
231 Mrs Janet W. Elliott
232 J. Stanton
233 Adelaide Janet Perks
234 Neil Radcliffe
235 A.C. Ashley
236 Kevin Loughrey
237 J.G. Watts
238 Joan Mary Scoble
239 James Stevens-Cox FSA
240 Eric F. Sandrey
241
242 Mrs M.I. Davies
243 D.M. Abbott
244 N.B.C. Patten
245 Molly & John Jennings
246 Darren G. Venus
247 A.J. Harvey
248 F.J.B. Denman
249 Ivor F. Russell
250 Bryan C. Tilzey
251 Harry S. Davey
252 Mrs Ruth Perry
253 C.A. Buchanan
254 Miss M.E.F. Cave
255 Valerie Deacon
256 Mrs Joan Ellen
    Gatehouse
257 Mr & Mrs E.J. Kinsman
258 D.N. Hadden
259 Julie Harrison
260 C.B. McVeigh
261 Mrs B.M. Lovering
262 John Coales
263 Mrs Carole A. Butler
264 Keith Douglas Woodham
265 Audrey K. Cox
266 Robert A. Hird
267 G. Windsor
268 John Lewis & Jennifer
    Hammond
269 Julian S. Freke
270 Hazel Singleton
271 Somerset Record Office
272 Veronica Turner
273 Mrs V. Willis
274 J.W. Sweet
275 Mrs T.J. Mintern
276 Mrs D.M. Norman
277 Mrs Patricia B. Cook JP
278 A. Whitty
279 Mrs A.R. Hardy
280 Lois M.W. Crisp
281 Mrs Dinah Cheek
282 R. Priddle
283 Kenneth Hince
284 John Curry
285 Clark Wyatt
286 Mrs Diana C. Redmond
287 George Edwin Frederick
288 Longhurst
289 Mrs V.H. Oaksford
290 Alan Perry
291 Mrs A. Thompson
292 The Rt Hon the Lord
    Rippon of Hexham QC
293 Dr A.B.M. McMaster
    BM MRCP
294
295 Mr & Mrs W.W. Chubb
296 Mr & Mrs J.E. Saunders
297 Desmond H.J. Danes
298 Michelle Nielson

299 Michael Murphy
300 D.L. Copeland-Eccles
301 Mrs J.M. Thorpe
302 K.S. Veryard
303 R.E. Ashurst
304 Mrs B. Wheeler
305 P.R. Burton
306 Mrs M. Ayres
307 Mrs B.A. Kingdon
308 W.H.S. Lush
309 R.N.A. Smith
310 D.A. Russell
311 Bucklers Mead School
    Library
312 Mrs J. Leveredge
313 Capt D.W. Ashby
    OBE RN
314 P.J. Reed
315 P.E. Paul
316 Mrs M.M. Leach
317 Mrs D.M. Lampard
318 Miss E.I.B. Taylor
319 D.F. Reid
320 Mrs C.J. Boucher
321 Mrs M.D. Pearce
322 Mrs Buckley
323 Mrs Joyce Cawthorne
324 Peter Sartin
325 Mr & Mrs M. Norris
326 Mr & Mrs R.J. Sinden
327 P.K. Burston
328 Mrs W.A. Quarterman
329 Mrs C.A. Laker
330 Robert Wilson
331 T.B. Smith
332 Mr & Mrs R.E. Peck
333 Mrs P.A. Stevens
334 Mrs Edna Smith
335 Miss S.R. McMillan
336 Miss J.R. Hockey
337 W.M. Winchester
338 D.J. Childs
339 Mrs K.M. Gibbons
340 C.T. Chubb
341 Mrs S.F. Taylor
342 Mrs B.M. Keech
343 Barry Sheridan
344 Mrs P. Stewart
345 Mr & Mrs N.J. Drake
346 C.C. Howell
347 Keith R. Stevens
348 Mrs M.J. Robbins
349 Mrs O.A. Pearce
350 Ivy E. Bayley
351 D.D.G. Frankland
352 Mrs D.M. Redward
353 Mrs J.E. Hipgrave
354 Mrs H. Penn
355 Ian Dunn
356 M. Hart
357 Miss E. Swain
358 R.H. Benjafield
359 Mrs J.E. Priddle
360 G.R. Hooper
361 Mr & Mrs S.R. Northover
362 R.I. Northover
363 K.J. Smith
364 Mrs P.J. Bishop
365 B.M. Codling
366 W.M. Craig
367 Mrs Violet Brewser
368 G.H. Bunting
369 Mrs B. Huggett

370 Roger Tostevin
371 David Adams
372 C. Stone
373 Mrs J. Jones
374 Jeremy Jones
375 Miss K.F. Smith
376 Mrs Katherine Barker
377 Mrs Jessie Riley
378 Dale Hockey
379 C.J. Holt
380 Mrs S.M. Russell
381 Jeffrey R. Wakeman
382 David Clive Merriman
383 Ruth Kendall
384 Yeofest 1990
385 Mandy Allen
386 Nancy Wills
387 Brian Edwards
388 Eric J.R. Bronn
389 Mrs C. Bentley
390 Judith Stocker
391 Mrs D. Shaw
392 G.J. & J.M. Humphrey
393 Mrs R.M.D. Stirling
394 David J. Leeper
395 Mr & Mrs M. Large
396 Mrs Q.C. Gardiner
397 K. Sims
398 Mr & Mrs P.J. Maddox
399 Mrs Mary Wilkinson
400 Mrs R.G. Hockey
401 Mrs C. Blyson
402 R.G. Clifton
403 Barry Rawlings
404 Mrs S.W. Rawlings
405 Mrs W. Andrews
406 Dawn Smith
407 M. Dietman
408 G.J. White
409 Bruce Grant King
410 Phyllis L. Waller
411 Mrs B.S. Aldridge
412 J. Carter
413 Mrs A. Rowsell
414 Clifford B. McVeigh
415 John Rowe
416 David Rowe
417 D.R. Morley
418 I.J. Holland
419 Isobel Pickard
420 R.S.A. Johnson
421 A.H. Jones
422 Kenneth John Newman
423 Mr & Mrs P. Magnus
424 Shirley Toogood
425 M. Dietman
426
427 R.A. Hoare
428 C. Close
429 A.D. Mountain
430 Robert Henry Thring
431 M.O. Shorey
432 J.A. Morley
433 D.R. Morley
434 A.J. Parsons
435 Capt G.D. Hinks
    TD FRSA
436 I.H.E. Ridout
437 W.E. Perry
438 R.W.T. Parker
439 Mrs M. Cole
440 Christine W. Helyar
441 D.W. Paulley

442 Mrs Margaret Burton
443 P.M. Street
444 Mrs E. Cross
445 K.B. Limrick
446 A.J.W. White
447 Mrs M.C. Lucas
448 Mrs H. Barnes
449 Mr & Mrs M.E. Pearce
450 Mr & Mrs K.J. Barber
451 C. Day
452 Mrs J. Glover
453 Raymond David Bush
454 Mrs Shelagh Brown
455 D.W. Eynon
456 Mrs H. Fletcher
457 Mrs J.A.E. Burgess
458 Mrs E. Vickery
459 J.W. Howarth
460 D.J. Drennan
461 F.P. Fen
462 J.R. Lane
463 Mrs V.I. Masters
464 Mrs M. Landry

465 K.W.G. Chainey
466 S. Birchell
467 Mrs N. Mullis
468 Mrs A.L. Paulley
469 Mrs I. Blackmore
470 S. Naylor
471 Mrs A. Hawkins
472 Mrs Y. Rake
473 Mr & Mrs H. Whalley
474 Clive & Linda Cooper
475 John Auriol Terrell
476 Rev E.J. Pulman
477 Dennis B. Wood
478 Douglas Melville Keyse
479 Paul John Warry
480 A.R. Woolmington
481 Mrs J. Frost
482 Mrs Anne Berkley
483 Mrs M.J. Barnett
484 A.D. Denslow
485 Pamela Brown
486 A. Whyman

487 David Brooks
488 Mr & Mrs P.D. Brooks
489 D.G. Barrett
490 Mrs E. Margaret Willy
491 Jeanne Margaret
       Beauchamp
492 Birchfield County
       Primary School
493 A.R. Brook
494 Hazel Gallimore'
495 B.R. Bergen
496 Martin Hamlin
497 Mrs J.K. Hallett
498 G.T. Leeson
499 Leslie Brooke
500 Mrs J. Hatcher
501 P.J. Bachrach
502 Mrs R. Lewis
503 L.G. Frost
504 Mrs E.A. Wookey
505 Alan Dawe
506 P. Taylor

507 Mrs M.E. Rothwell
508 J. Gilbert
509 A.W. Grossam
510 Mrs H. Elkin
511 Jonathan Trevett
512 Cheryl Jensen
513 H.R.L. Spurrier
514 C.H. Marks
515 Margaret Alice Hudson
516 Rhona Parry
517 Mrs S.A. Tucker
518 C.W.J. Woodsford
519 Avril & Andrew Stallard
520 Eric M. Garrett
521 Mrs H.J. Woodridge
522 Mrs J. Brookman
523 S. Thomas Pickles
524 D.G. Andrews
525 Malcolm Bull
526 Mr & Mrs J.G. Hayes
527 D.A.E. Maclaren
528 B. Stainer
529 G.E. Templeman

Remaining names unlisted

140

North-east section of Yeovil 1831, redrawn and adapted from a survey by E. Watts.